The Chemistry of Personality

A GUIDE TO TEACHER-STUDENT INTERACTION IN THE CLASSROOM

ELIZABETH MURPHY

Center for Applications of Psychological Type · Gainesville, FL 32609 · 800.777.2278 (USA and Canada) · www.capt.org

Published by

Center for Applications of Psychological Type, Inc.

2815 NW 13th Street, Suite 401

Gainesville, FL 32609

352.375.0160

www.capt.org

Center for Applications of Psychological Type, Inc. and CAPT are trademarks or registered trademarks of the Center for Applications of Psychological Type in the United States and other countries.

Murphy-Meisgeier Type Indicator for Children and MMTIC are trademarks or registered trademarks of Elizabeth Murphy and Charles Meisgeier in the United States and other countries.

Myers-Briggs Type Indicator, Myers-Briggs, and MBTI are trademarks or registered trademarks of the Myers-Briggs Type Indicator Trust in the United States and other countries.

Murphy, Elizabeth, 1949-
  The chemistry of personality : a guide to teacher-student interaction in the classroom / Elizabeth Murphy.
      p. cm.
  Includes bibliographical references.
  ISBN-13: 978-0-935652-82-6 (pbk.)
  ISBN-10: 0-935652-82-5 (pbk.)
  1. Typology (Psychology) 2. Personality. 3. Cognitive styles. 4. Learning, Psychology of. 5. Teachers--Psychology. 6. Students--Psychology. I. Title.
  BF698.3M87 2008

  370.15'32--dc22

2008012857

TABLE OF CONTENTS

PREFACE

There are many models to explain differences in learning styles among students, and teachers explore these to discover the best ways to meet the needs of their students. Of all models I have studied, psychological type is the one that seems most complete. This model defines normal differences in the ways information is processed and the ways people make decisions, as well as their styles of interacting in the world. Using type concepts with students enriches my instructional day and facilitates the achievement levels of the students I teach. Professionals tend to share tools that work well for them. The education profession is a sharing profession. With this work I hope to share with you how type can be constructively used to enhance educational opportunities for students and how an understanding of your teaching style can help you enjoy the various styles of fellow teachers, who can also bring a unique approach to learning for students.

Cognizant of the limited time that teachers often have for their enrichment, I have written this booklet in a way that introduces and explains type in an easy-to-follow and succinct manner. You will be introduced to style differences in teaching, as well as information about the differences in the ways students process information and make decisions. Suggestions for working with these differences provide the educator with practices to immediately implement the concepts of psychological type in the classroom.

The goal is not to make a perfect world for each learner but to understand the variety of options available to help learners manage their styles and reach their objectives. An instructional objective should always be maintained but offering a variety of ways to meet that objective recognizes the natural diversity that exists in human nature that educators want to encourage.

The development of the personality proceeds over time. The younger the learner, the less likely they are able to adapt to the task when the task does not match their style. Teachers of elementary students recognize they need to be flexible because developmentally children at that level do not have multiple tools for processing information. As these skills develop, the students become more adept at accommodating the demands of different style tasks and by high school students are developing a better balance in these skills. Still they need to understand their best ways of learning and relating so they can effectively manage their energies to work on tasks that do not match their innate style. Understanding type concepts helps educators plan for a variety of choices in their classes that let students stretch to learn new skills while using their strengths to master difficult concepts.

By casting a wide net of possible learning approaches, teachers can more easily snare students into the web of success. Using type concepts has been the most effective tool for me to help accomplish this goal. I share it with you in hope that it will offer you the same experience.

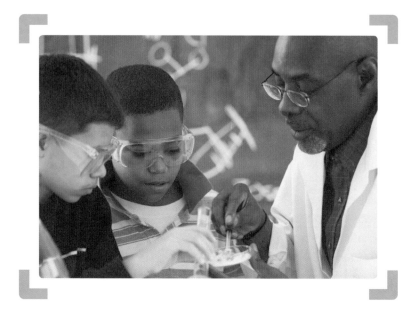

The goal is not to make a perfect
world for each learner but to understand
the variety of options available to
help learners manage their styles and
reach their objectives.

1

Understanding Type in the Classroom

A person's psychological type is a profile of his or her preferred ways of being. According to Jung's lifetime developmental theory, we are born with a predisposition to favor one profile over other potential profiles. When we use our preferences, tasks feel easier and more natural, and we welcome opportunities to engage in tasks that play to our skills. When we are required to use a less preferred approach, perhaps because of situational expectations, we can do so but it takes more energy, and is initially more difficult, and we are often glad when that portion of the task is completed.

I enjoy competition. I will try to have more fun while I'm competing and not be so serious about it so my friends won't get mad. (ESTJ)

The Myers-Briggs Type Indicator® (MBTI®) instrument is used to measure type preferences in adults. The MBTI instrument is used worldwide and applies to personal development across multiple disciplines (families, education, business, multicultural, and more). It is often referred to as the most widely used instrument for normal personality assessment.

The Murphy-Meisgeier Type Indicator® (MMTIC™) assessment is used to measure type preferences in students in grades two through twelve. The MMTIC instrument helps students to identify the strengths and stretches that come about from their preferred ways of approaching people, tasks, and their environments. The MMTIC takes approximately thirty minutes to administer and can be taken independently online or with paper and pencil. Results can be shared individually or in classes.

About Personality Type

Personality type is about energy that is innate. It does not predict how a person will behave. According to MBTI theory, people can choose to change their behaviors, but they cannot change the source of energy that comes from their type preferences. Behavior is a choice. The source of energy is not.

Awareness of type encourages people to . . .

• better understand themselves.

• better understand others.

• manage energy and talents.

• value the talents of others even if they are different.

Type preference is not related to competence. A person can use nonpreferred skills to competently complete a task; however the task may take more energy than completing a task that better matches their preferences.

Value of Type Awareness in Education

Understanding type has benefits for teachers and students. When students are taught type concepts, they can learn to manage study habits better, recognize their patterns of learning, and manage relationship skills. When teachers learn and apply type concepts, they are better able to manage their energy for teaching, structure instruction to accommodate the differences between individual students, and adapt assessments to more accurately measure learning. No instructional objective is sacrificed in order to accommodate these differences. Style of learning is addressed rather than the substance of the learning activity.

Type awareness in an educational setting can help in the following ways:

• Improve classroom climate.

• Help promote individual achievement.

• Facilitate team building among teachers.

• Encourage individual responsibility for learning.

• Provide a framework for lesson design that accommodates all learning approaches.

• Provide a framework for designing assessment methods that account for differences.

Students need to both think and feel that the classroom is a place that honors their various styles. Providing for differences means that greater numbers of students will be able to succeed in the classroom environment.

To help students adapt and learn based on an awareness of type differences teachers need to be able to do the following:

• Know the natural differences expressed by different types.

• Know what a situation requires and ask such questions as, "Is this a time for action or reflection?" or "Does this step of a task require details or looking at the big picture?" People can behave any way necessary, but the energy each personality needs to match the situation is quite different.

• Facilitate the merger between the child and the situation. Facilitation bridges the gap between what the child naturally knows and does well and what is required at the moment.

Knowledge of type is an adjunct to the skills that you have already built as an education professional. Before using type concepts, you should know your subject matter, understand the general concepts of lesson preparation and presentation, and be willing to adjust lessons to accommodate normal differences. First you must create a sound basis for instruction, and then you can incorporate type concepts into your program.

Type offers teachers . . .

• a framework for differentiating curriculum.

• opportunities for developing strategies that honor differences in the classroom.

• more relaxed classrooms as learners engage with the lessons.

• more productive environments as learners manage their energy and behavior.

The Type Scales

Four dichotomous scales, described here, make up the basis of psychological type.

Living Differences
(How a person interacts with information and with others is noticed in daily interactions)

Extraversion or Introversion

Judging or Perceiving

Communication and Information Processing Differences

Sensing or Intuition

Relationship and Decision-Making Differences

Thinking or Feeling

MMTIC Preference Icons © 2008 Center for Applications of Psychological Type

When students are taught type
concepts, they can learn to
manage study habits better,
recognize their patterns of learning,
and manage relationship skills.

2

General Descriptions of the Eight Preferences

The following general type descriptions identify the preferred ways people might select for processing information and making decisions. These are just some examples of type descriptions and the reflection of that preference in a teaching style.

Type Descriptions—Extraversion and Introversion

Extraverts

- Find that talking helps thinking.
- Are energized by doing.
- Like short "wait time" before responding.
- Are inclined to express emotion when hurt, angry, or upset.
- Require quiet to concentrate when the work is difficult.

Introverts

- Think first, then share.
- Are energized by time alone.
- Like longer wait time before responding.
- Have difficulty expressing emotion when hurt, angry, or upset.
- Enjoy quiet, but can focus and concentrate when necessary.

Teaching Differences with Extraversion and Introversion

Extraverted Teachers

- Enjoy active classrooms—energy is "out there." The teacher may need to tell the class to quiet down at times.
- Prefer minimal time between question and answers in discussions.
- May judge classroom participation based on who spoke or on outward behaviors.
- May try to engage a student by asking questions and offering suggestions.

Introverted Teachers

- Tend to value "quiet" classrooms.
- May offer more independent assignments.
- May wait longer between questions and answers.
- May not feel like socializing at the end of the day.

Type Descriptions—Sensing and Intuition

Sensing Types

- Prefer using skills already learned.
- Prefer the definite and measurable.
- Rely on experience to understand concepts.
- Notice details.
- Recall facts and specific information.
- Seem to memorize well.
- Value precise directions.
- Like to study the real and the practical.
- May get bogged down in details.

Intuitive Types

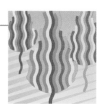

- Focus more on the theme or whole than on the parts.
- Focus on the future—What else? What's new?
- Tend to focus on possibilities rather than on what is real.
- Learn best with variety in the presentation.
- Enjoy designing projects more than doing them.
- Prefer to study new skills rather than rehearse or repeat learned skills.
- May skip over facts or get them wrong because they focused on forming connections.

Teaching Differences with Sensing and Intuition

Sensing Teachers

- Tend to use multiple examples to demonstrate a point.
- May require students to complete various assignments to demonstrate learning of previously introduced concepts.
- May develop assessment tools that measure the recall of information in specific and detailed ways.
- Provide directions for tasks and uses specific details as the frame for assignments.
- Provide information in small units to allow learners time to process and file information before continuing on to new content.

Intuitive Teachers

- Value teaching with stories and themes, symbolic connections, and metaphors.
- Use their intuition to expand on ideas that develop during a discussion.
- May develop thematic lesson or use theme units from month to month.
- Might rely on essay tests or creative projects as a method of assessing learning.
- May try to inspire students by brainstorming all possible themes or connections and providing open-ended options.

Type Descriptions—Thinking and Feeling

Thinking Types

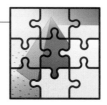

- Value independence.
- Enjoy competition.
- Ask why?
- Use logic to solve problems.
- Like the challenge of solving problems.
- Need recognition for their accomplishments.
- Evaluate their performance then seek feedback.

Feeling Types

- Need to feel connected.
- Try to please others.
- Enjoy helping others.
- Make choices that honor their values.
- May ignore personal needs while taking care of others.
- Need appreciation for their service.
- Like feedback from others before evaluating self.

Teaching Differences with Thinking and Feeling

Thinking Teachers

- Value mastery.
- Use critical feedback more than supportive feedback to help the learner.
- Maintain the standard of learning in the classroom.
- Value fairness in the classroom.

Feeling Teachers

- Value effort.
- Use supportive feedback more than critical feedback to help the learner.
- Like cooperative groups.
- Praise frequently.
- Address multiple needs of learners.

Type Descriptions—Judging and Perceiving

Judging Types

- Prefer completing one project before beginning another.
- Do not want to reconsider an issue, once a decision is made.
- Enjoy structure and predictability.
- Appreciate a schedule to follow.
- Work best when work can be planned and the plan can be followed.
- Prefer to control the world by planning for possibilities.
- Seem to have a natural ability to manage time.

Perceiving Types

- Find joy in experiencing projects and may not have the need to finish them.
- Seem to act spontaneously.
- Try to incorporate fun with work.
- Seem to enjoy the "doing" part of activities more than the end product.
- Handle unexpected changes well.
- Prefer to control their world by adapting to events as they occur.
- Like to keep options open until a decision must be made.

Teaching Differences with Judging and Perceiving

Judging Teachers

- Plan ahead and want to follow the plan.
- Want to reach decisions and to resolve questions quickly.
- Value preparation and usually is well-prepared.
- Tend to separate work and play so that opportunities for fun and play follow the completion of tasks or assignments.

Perceiving Teachers

- Value flexibility and may be so flexible that the day is not planned completely.
- May not finish all the projects they start.
- Support activities that incorporate fun in the learning sequence.
- May get absorbed in the lesson and lose track of time.

Understanding type concepts
helps educators plan for a variety of
choices in their classes that let
students stretch to learn new
skills while using their strengths
to master difficult concepts.

3

Teacher Types

When teachers understand their preferred styles of classroom organization, lesson presentation, and assessment, as well as the variety of needs of students in their classes, they will have optimal skills for addressing learning preferences among their students. On the following pages are descriptions of the sixteen types of teaching styles.

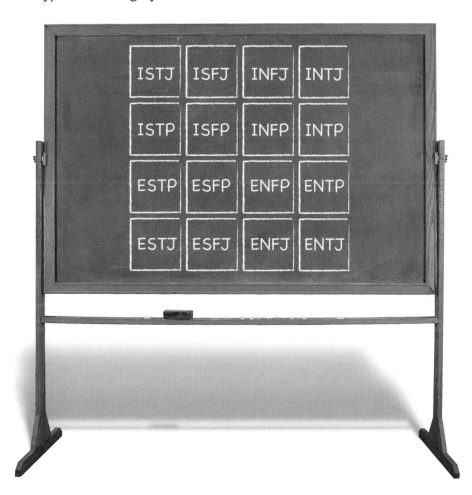

Teacher Types ISTJ

ISTJ teachers enjoy students who . . .

- follow the rules.
- read and use textbooks and materials.
- submit their work on time.
- set personal goals and make plans to meet those goals.
- support their ideas with specific facts and examples.

ISTJ teachers are challenged by students who . . .

- fail to complete scheduled assignments on time.
- talk about doing work but don't actually get it done.
- think of possibilities that go beyond the reality of what they can reasonably produce.
- need feedback to understand if they are doing well.

ISTJ teachers believe education should . . .

- pass on relevant information to future generations.
- teach learners how to identify the real problem.
- teach learners how to use the past to find solutions or to adapt present ways to find solutions.
- prepare students for the ability to think on their own.

ISTJ teachers design lessons that . . .

- have a logical sequence.
- explain the cause and effect.
- present a problem and a way to solve it.
- use several supporting examples to prove a point.
- are paced to be finished in the allotted time.

ISTJ teachers are most excited about a school organization that . . .

- has goals and a plan to meet those goals.
- focuses on one or two achievable goals rather than many.
- uses data to validate learning and justify changes.
- allows teachers to work independently if they get the job done.

ISTJ teachers are most tested by other teachers who . . .

- are disorganized.
- talk about ideas but don't implement those ideas.
- violate rules and cause others to be inconvenienced.

ISTJ teachers are most effective when they . . .

- know the plan.
- work on their own.
- can prove their students are learning.

Teacher Types ISFJ

ISFJ teachers enjoy students who . . .

- are patient and wait their turns.
- do not question authority unnecessarily.
- do not ask why they need to know something.
- work to please and appreciate extra help.
- practice to learn how to do work well.

ISFJ teachers are challenged by students who . . .

- become easily frustrated and don't want to listen to the steps to be followed.
- expect to master a concept quickly and jump to conclusions.
- talk over other classmates and don't listen to others.
- argue with you if you don't agree with what they say.

ISFJ teachers believe education should . . .

- make the student aware of others and appreciate differences in people.
- build self-confidence.
- help students connect with fellow humanity.
- prepare students to learn skills that will help them function in life.

ISFJ teachers design lessons that . . .

- allow for practice of a concept that flows into creative additions or adaptations.
- allow time for introspection and reflection before group interaction.
- begin with the facts and build a case for the general concept.

- use several supporting examples to demonstrate a concept.
- allow students to work together as peer tutors when appropriate.

ISFJ teachers are most excited about a school organization that . . .

- allows for personal freedom to teach the best way for their style.
- provides support when needed (with tasks, families, or students).
- has a set of clear expectations.
- applies rules equally to all teachers and students.

ISFJ teachers are most tested by other teachers who . . .

- think their subject is the most important and are not flexible with others.
- wait until the last moment to plan lessons that involve others.
- violate rules and cause others to be inconvenienced.

ISFJ teachers are most effective when they . . .

- feel they are appreciated for their dedication and service.
- feel that others have confidence in them.
- have the materials they need and the opportunity to thrive in their classes.

Teacher Types INFJ

INFJ teachers enjoy students who . . .

- listen to directions and follow classroom rules.

- show an interest in and excitement about learning new information.

- show respect by cooperating with others.

- complete assignments on time.

- find new and exciting ways to present projects or essays.

INFJ teachers are challenged by students who . . .

- disrupt the learning of others.

- ask questions for specific information that is not readily available.

- resist following the classroom routine.

- must prove they are right when there is disagreement.

INFJ teachers believe education should . . .

- help all students to learn at their level.

- improve the condition of the world—socially, economically, and politically.

- help students to find their special talents in the world.

- inspire students to take risks wisely.

INFJ teachers design lessons that . . .

- encourage students to explore components that interest them most.

- are structured for further exploration.

- begin with an issue and then help students find the information they need to solve the problem.

- are individualized.

- are light-hearted and leave time for student questions.

INFJ teachers are most excited about a school organization that . . .

- supports the teacher in any way needed.

- is willing to take risks and try new ways of teaching to help individual students.

- honors some traditions but is comfortable exploring new ways to celebrate those traditions.

- allows teachers to work independently if they get the job done.

INFJ teachers are most tested by other teachers who . . .

- fail to share good ideas with others so they can be the best.

- don't teach, let the student get behind, and thus create wide gaps between learners for the next year.

- say they are spontaneous but really just don't plan effectively.

INFJ teachers are most effective when they . . .

- have the resources and time to prepare lessons well.

- have students committed to the learning process.

- have the support and assistance of other teachers on their team who work well together.

Teacher Types **INTJ**

INTJ teachers enjoy students who . . .

- ask clarifying questions that require new or more information.
- are prepared for class.
- work independently competently.
- allow others to speak or work without interruption.
- are creative and original but focused on an ultimate goal.

INTJ teachers are challenged by students who . . .

- don't listen to others (teacher or students).
- are confrontational and defiant.
- enjoy derailing the lesson with antics and silliness.
- think out loud without respect for other learners.

INTJ teachers believe education should . . .

- teach students how to learn.
- enhance skills as a means to becoming a lifelong learner.
- give students a foundation to build upon.
- challenge current concepts and explore new possibilities.

INTJ teachers design lessons that . . .

- test and analyze.
- are logical.
- start with the big picture and fill in the details.
- challenge students to find an answer that may not be in the book.
- are based on the opinions of experts.

INTJ teachers are most excited about a school organization that . . .

- gives them freedom to show creativity.
- allows them to run their classrooms as they think best.
- bases educational decisions on theories of learning.
- allows teachers to work independently if they get the job done.

INTJ teachers are most tested by other teachers who . . .

- need a lot of details up front prior to getting on board with an idea.
- talk about self-esteem issues over achievement issues.
- focus on the fun in a lesson but don't have a clear concept of the material to be learned.

INTJ teachers are most effective when they . . .

- have a clear goal and are given a vote of confidence to accomplish it.
- are allowed to prove their students are learning.
- can use less conventional methods so long as they prove the effectiveness of their approach.

Teacher Types ISTP

ISTP teachers enjoy students who . . .

- work independently with clear directions.
- feel free to laugh and enjoy learning while they finish their work.
- want to learn the how and why of lessons.
- can explain the justification for their answers.
- use details to prove their points.

ISTP teachers are challenged by students who . . .

- are afraid to work independently for fear they will make a mistake.
- get irritated when a schedule is changed.
- have ideas but no clue how to make those ideas real.
- need to interact with others seemingly all the time.

ISTP teachers believe education should . . .

- be exciting.
- include some trial and error learning.
- teach students to solve problems logically and quickly by manipulating data and materials.
- prepare students to solve their own problems.

ISTP teachers design lessons that . . .

- teach students how to break lessons into their component parts and note how these relate to each other.
- encourage students to use materials and previous knowledge to solve problems.

- are active and hands-on.
- include a demonstration to get the students started on the right track.
- include challenging contests to demonstrate learned skills.

ISTP teachers are most excited about a school organization that . . .

- has sufficient materials for all students.
- encourages teacher autonomy in each classroom rather than similarities among team members.
- is flexible with curriculum or procedures to accommodate the learners.
- recognizes the need for students to have time to work through a concept.

ISTP teachers are most tested by other teachers who . . .

- promote a consistent routine over the needs of the moment.
- emphasize using rules and regulations to change the environment.
- bring emotions about personal issues into the learning environment.

ISTP teachers are most effective when they . . .

- can be adventurous and humorous with their style of teaching.
- work on their own.
- are challenged and given the necessary materials to meet that challenge.

Teacher Types ISFP

ISFP teachers enjoy students who . . .

- like classrooms that are spontaneous and have surprise experiences.
- generate enthusiasm for the task or the learning.
- are cooperative with other students and do not let their personal freedom interfere with others.
- can work independently.
- show appreciation for extra help.

ISFP teachers are challenged by students who . . .

- cannot work in a room with a lot of activity.
- start a task without understanding the directions.
- do not follow through with minor details.
- fail to show appreciation for teachers and peers.

ISFP teachers believe education should . . .

- help students develop an appreciation for the beauty of life.
- encourage students to enjoy what they are doing while they do it.
- help students discover their own values in a supportive environment.
- be fun, experiential, and exciting.

ISFP teachers design lessons that . . .

- include elements of art, music, and/or drama.
- include sensory experiences.
- include playful yet cooperative games.
- require students to be actively involved in the learning.
- include an element of surprise.

ISFP teachers are most excited about a school organization that . . .

- endorses personal freedom in the classroom.
- reduces paperwork for teachers.
- appreciates and affirms teachers for their dedication and service.
- is flexible with schedules when possible.

ISFP teachers are most tested by other teachers who . . .

- plan and want only that plan to be used.
- do not follow through with their promises.
- have excessive noise in a classroom that is seen as a sign of poor classroom control.

ISFP teachers are most effective when they . . .

- are faced with an emergency and need to respond quickly.
- are encouraged to allow students to explore their world and to play while they learn.
- focus on learning rather than on paperwork.

Teacher Types INFP

INFP teachers enjoy students who . . .

- care about the world and about other students.
- get to know teachers beyond the limits of the classroom.
- believe in a cause and work to support that cause.
- bend the rules but complete the assignments.
- think and care about others in the class.

INFP teachers are challenged by students who . . .

- need things repeated multiple times.
- have a need to always be active.
- shut down when work appears difficult.
- notice what is wrong first and fail to mention what is right.

INFP teachers believe education should . . .

- give all students a comparable chance for success in life.
- provide individual challenges.
- build citizens for the future.
- be flexible.

INFP teachers design lessons that . . .

- can be individualized.
- have a game-like and playful nature incorporated into the lesson.
- start with a tantalizing story or issue and lead to an understanding of the concepts.
- incorporate current events.
- allow students to offer divergent answers.

INFP teachers are most excited about a school organization that . . .

- is on the forefront of what is effective in educational services.
- respects the individuality of the teacher and the student.
- rewards and recognizes teachers who achieve their objectives.
- incorporates the resources (human and financial) of the community into the school.
- allows teachers to teach flexible lessons rather than a lock-step curriculum.

INFP teachers are most tested by other teachers who . . .

- put down any new idea because they are too busy.
- fail to follow through with expectations.
- fail to help individual children under the guise that it is the student's obligation to catch up.

INFP teachers are most effective when they . . .

- feel they are a valued member of the learning community.
- are not pressed for completing numerous paperwork requirements.
- can explore learning with students without always having to assess them.

Teacher Types **INTP**

INTP teachers enjoy students who . . .

- rise to the high standards they set.
- think outside the box.
- challenge and make them see things from a perspective not yet examined.
- work independently when appropriate and participate in a group when expected.
- explore multiple facets of a theory.
- show respect to their peers and are willing to take risks.

INTP teachers are challenged by students who . . .

- need step-by-step directions.
- won't generate their own ideas for projects and assignments.
- give up without trying a variety of strategies to approach a project.
- need frequent praise and feedback to function.

INTP teachers believe education should . . .

- challenge the learner.
- stimulate new thinking.
- foster the individual to think for themselves for the purpose of improving humanity.
- encourage independence.

INTP teachers design lessons that . . .

- appeal to the use of strategies.
- tend to be atypical in their approach.
- encourage students to learn on their own.
- start with the theory and explore supporting details.

- intertwine multiple factors to explain complex phenomena.
- are constructive and support a grander scheme to explain how parts come together.

INTP teachers are most excited about a school organization that . . .

- leaves them to their own devices.
- pushes them to produce more.
- is open to progressive styles, as well as traditional styles of teaching.
- lets the classroom operate at the discretion of the teacher.
- encourages collegiality.

INTP teachers are most tested by other teachers who . . .

- are inflexible.
- are brusque or resistant to options.
- are resistant to myriad approaches to a subject or are not open to different styles.

INTP teachers are most effective when they . . .

- are engaged in framing the instructional system.
- have input for the idea phase.
- study or practice on their own and then present their findings to the group.
- are under constant pressure to perform.

Teacher Types ESTP

ESTP teachers enjoy students who . . .

- have a sense of humor.
- are active participants in the class.
- think through an issue by carefully considering necessary information.
- engage in active debate with data to prove their point.
- can laugh at themselves when they make a mistake.

ESTP teachers are challenged by students who . . .

- work slowly.
- don't advocate for themselves.
- get upset when given critical feedback.
- want to know well in advance what the scheduled learning will be.

ESTP teachers believe education should . . .

- be exciting while teaching basic skills.
- be accessible to all students.
- require students to formulate new thought.
- require students to understand the past in order to design for the future.

ESTP teachers design lessons that . . .

- are active and use multiple explanations.
- provide variety, using demonstrations and hands-on lessons.
- are interactive.
- prove the concept by game or activity.
- require learning outside the classroom in order to participate in the activity in the room.

ESTP teachers are most excited about a school organization that . . .

- allows for personal freedom.
- has a well-developed curriculum.
- encourages students to take action beyond the classroom.
- supports the value of action learning rather than testing for knowledge.

ESTP teachers are most tested by other teachers who . . .

- are verbose without making any significant point.
- are inflexible with schedules, tasks, or styles.
- see noise in a classroom as a lack of control.

ESTP teachers are most effective when they . . .

- are given freedom to instruct using their style.
- set a high bar.
- are allowed to interact with the students and materials to promote learning.

Teacher Types ESFP

ESFP teachers enjoy students who . . .

- are excited about learning.
- have similar strong values.
- listen to directions and pick up specifics.
- ask for help when needed.
- turn in work on time.

ESFP teachers are challenged by students who . . .

- fail to ask for help and then get frustrated.
- can never find things.
- miss things because they didn't listen to details.
- try to do things so differently that it is unclear whether they learned the critical elements.

ESFP teachers believe education should . . .

- encourage students to be their best.
- make students feel good about themselves while they develop basic skills.
- challenge students to discover what is important to them.
- meet the needs of all students as individual learners.

ESFP teachers design lessons that . . .

- are group oriented.
- require an awareness of details.
- have a game-like nature or a playfulness that enhances the lesson.

- are spontaneous adaptations of a general plan.
- allow learners a chance to work with each other and learn from each other.

ESFP teachers are most excited about a school organization that . . .

- allows all students to feel welcome and gives individual feedback.
- has predictable leadership that is consistent and equitable where all teachers feel valued.
- celebrates different learning styles.
- has a structure in the school that builds in success for all students.

ESFP teachers are most tested by other teachers who . . .

- are rigid about deadlines.
- dismiss their ideas or their questions as not important to the theme.
- don't realize their comments are hurtful.

ESFP teachers are most effective when they . . .

- are able to teach in the way that works best for them.
- are trusted to be successful with students.
- feel valued and appreciated for their efforts.

Teacher Types ENFP

ENFP teachers enjoy students who . . .

- are involved.
- participate in class discussions with new ideas and new questions.
- are helpful and generous.
- develop a new and different approach to their work.
- connect current learning with previous learning.

ENFP teachers are challenged by students who . . .

- are quiet and unresponsive.
- do not ask for help or need their constant help.
- never laugh.
- want to follow the schedule and find it difficult to adapt at the last moment.

ENFP teachers believe education should . . .

- be interactive.
- be enjoyable.
- be informative.
- be a format for designing changes that will impact the student's future.

ENFP teachers design lessons that . . .

- are active and fun.
- allow students to have an emotional connection to thinking.
- allow students to share information if they choose.

- encourage students to go beyond the text.
- ask students to integrate multiple topics under a common theme.

ENFP teachers are most excited about a school organization that . . .

- allows all teachers to excel.
- sticks to standards but lets teachers find various ways to meet those standards.
- views the school as a community of learners with multiple perspectives.
- encourages teachers to team together for the good of the whole.

ENFP teachers are most tested by other teachers who . . .

- are not involved and do not participate in faculty gatherings.
- have lost their enthusiasm for teaching.
- are very concrete or only see one way to accomplish a task.

ENFP teachers are most effective when they . . .

- can generate and review information as a group.
- have freedom to teach in the way that works best for them and for their students.
- are given positive feedback about their contribution to the school and the community.

The Chemistry of Personality: A Guide to Teacher-Student Interaction in the Classroom

Teacher Types ENTP

ENTP teachers enjoy students who . . .

- want to explore the complicated possibilities.
- can be flexible with schedules and plans.
- think outside the box.
- follow through with the ideas they think have value.
- recognize and acknowledge the expertise of the teacher.

ENTP teachers are challenged by students who . . .

- need information repeated.
- get caught up with specifics before understanding the idea.
- are afraid to take risks and look to the policies and procedures for answers.
- keep their ideas quiet until it is too late.

ENTP teachers believe education should . . .

- stimulate the mind to new insights and action.
- stretch the brightest students and help all students to learn.
- go beyond the classroom and extend into the world.
- be exciting for the learner.

ENTP teachers design lessons that . . .

- pose problems to be solved.
- challenge current ways of thinking about a problem.

- have no single correct answer.
- are involved and take a few sessions to complete.
- use data in unconventional ways.

ENTP teachers are most excited about a school organization that . . .

- respects their autonomy.
- allows each teacher freedom but holds each teacher accountable for student success.
- measures success in the classroom by more than a standard score on a test.
- encourages the growth of the staff as well as the growth of the students.

ENTP teachers are most tested by other teachers who . . .

- want every answer resolved before proceeding.
- bring up rules as a reason for not doing something.
- ask thousands of clarifying questions but never offer new ideas.

ENTP teachers are most effective when they . . .

- act independently.
- have resources at their disposal for research and investigation.
- work with students who like to be challenged to discover learning.

Teacher Types ESTJ

ESTJ teachers enjoy students who . . .

- can learn from the past.
- are able to support their positions with multiple examples.
- meet schedules and commitments without reminder.
- can analyze a problem and know what data is needed to solve the problem.
- find new possibilities by exploring what was previously done and modifying creatively.

ESTJ teachers are challenged by students who . . .

- expect the teacher to entertain them.
- are extremely needy with questions or wanting feedback about their performance.
- refuse to speak in class but then want to ask questions after class.
- offer ideas but do not have the information to support them.

ESTJ teachers believe education should . . .

- seek to meet all the needs of the child— social, emotional, academic.
- be consistent; sequential building of skills across grades.
- hold students accountable for mastery of basic skills.
- provide adequate resources for each student to learn (e.g. lab equipment, computers).

ESTJ teachers design lessons that . . .

- are varied—i.e., short activities, longer projects.

- have straight-forward directions.
- balance independent activities with group work.
- build on one another and include set rewards or praise for mastering specific goals.
- have an identified outcome to be met.

ESTJ teachers are most excited about a school organization that . . .

- supports teachers and students.
- has class rules/expectations—stands up to parents and enforces consequences.
- gathers data to document performance of teachers and students.
- respects and celebrates school traditions.

ESTJ teachers are most tested by other teachers who . . .

- seem unorganized and waste time in meetings.
- look at their needs and not the needs of all.
- say they are going to do something and then fail to meet that obligation.

ESTJ teachers are most effective when they . . .

- are first given an outline and framework of clear criteria and then allowed to work on their own.
- know the standard that is to be met.
- have the flexibility to challenge themselves to exceed the expectations.

Teacher Types ESFJ

ESFJ teachers enjoy students who . . .

- are excited about learning.
- show effort.
- have a good attitude.
- work well with their classmates.
- learn supporting facts first to discover new possibilities.

ESFJ teachers are challenged by students who . . .

- have no system for organization.
- miss significant details in the lecture and in directions.
- talk about a lot of ideas but fail to produce.
- challenge every observation and want to know why before working.

ESFJ teachers believe education should . . .

- meet the needs of all children.
- teach lifelong skills.

- teach students to be lifelong learners.
- be a stable and unifying force in the community for sharing with each other.

ESFJ teachers design lessons that . . .

- reach all students including the slow and the bright.
- are sequential and build on previous learning.
- are personal.
- emphasize directly the content to be learned.
- can be completed in the allotted time.

ESFJ teachers are most excited about a school organization that . . .

- gives feedback that is personal.
- celebrates differences.
- has predictable leadership that is consistent and fair.
- creates a community of colleagues.

ESFJ teachers are most tested by other teachers who . . .

- don't follow agreed upon time schedules.
- fail to take the obligations of others seriously.
- seek change without a real reason.

ESFJ teachers are most effective when they . . .

- have an environment that is conflict free or a working system for resolving conflict.
- have programs and expectations that are consistent.
- feel appreciated and valued for their efforts.

Teacher Types ENFJ

ENFJ teachers enjoy students who . . .

- follow directions.
- participate—share their ideas.
- work together as a community of learners.
- enjoy exploring new possibilities.
- make decisions and help teams reach closure.

ENFJ teachers are challenged by students who . . .

- are unfocused on the current task.
- believe they have all the answers and have to wait for the class to catch up.
- criticize the current assignments but offer no acceptable alternative.
- have needs but never ask for help.

ENFJ teachers believe education should . . .

- reach all students.
- increase knowledge.
- examine social attitudes and behavior.
- produce citizens capable of independent thought but who are also committed to the community of people.

ENFJ teachers design lessons that . . .

- try to reach everyone.
- include discussion and encourage students to share learning and ideas verbally.
- put a different slant on a familiar topic to keep the learning fresh.
- offer choices.
- encourage team projects as well as independent projects.

ENFJ teachers are most excited about a school organization that . . .

- teaches tolerance and understanding.
- encourages staff and students to reach their personal best.
- recognizes the need for a variety of options to meet the various learning levels of students.
- cares about the students as well as the test scores of the students.

ENFJ teachers are most tested by other teachers who . . .

- change the direction often.
- fail to take action in a timely way.
- tell you what is wrong but don't try to make it right.

ENFJ teachers are most effective when they . . .

- work with people who are focused and task driven.
- have the freedom to try a variety of ways to solve a problem.
- are appreciated for their dedication to the students.

Teacher Types ENTJ

ENTJ teachers enjoy students who . . .

- like to get things done.
- are organized.
- are to the point.
- are quick to see the flaw in a plan.
- are willing to take risks to discover new insights.

ENTJ teachers are challenged by students who . . .

- repeatedly present the same problem without any thought for solving it.
- complain.
- are too quiet.
- don't follow the schedule.

ENTJ teachers believe education should . . .

- be fun as well as useful.
- serve a purpose.
- help you succeed.
- give you inner direction as well as worldly accomplishments.

ENTJ teachers design lessons that . . .

- keep students motivated by challenging their thinking.
- encourage independent projects.
- pose a problem and help learners find multiple solutions.
- start with the theory and then document support of that theory.
- encourage all students to stretch to a new level.

ENTJ teachers are most excited about a school organization that . . .

- ranks number one.
- investigates new technology and ideas.
- has a hands-off administrator.
- has high expectations.

ENTJ teachers are most tested by other teachers who . . .

- take too long to explain things.
- appear disorganized.
- are unapproachable or appear offended when their idea is challenged.

ENTJ teachers are most effective when they . . .

- work independently.
- know what needs to be done and are given the freedom to get it done.
- create a system for delivering information effectively.

When teachers learn and apply
type concepts, they are better able to
manage their energy for teaching,
structure instruction to accommodate
the differences between individual
students, and adapt assessments to more
accurately measure learning.

4

Student's Strengths and Stretches

Students bring their own type of strengths and stretches to a learning situation. Tasks that match their strengths will appear easy. Tasks that match their least-preferred approach will appear to be more difficult and will take more energy to execute successfully. These will be their stretches. The following pages provide examples of each type's strengths and stretches.

Strengths & Stretches ISTJ

(Practical Analyzer)

When ISTJs use their preferred style they . . .

- Complete tasks with attention to detail.
- Have a practical and organized way of describing critical information.
- Use sufficient facts to support their ideas.
- Follow through and complete what needs to be done.
- Look to the past for ideas to solve present problems effectively.
- Analyze for cause and effect to clarify a situation.
- Clarify by asking pertinent questions.
- Lead others to practical applications through their thorough analysis.

ISTJ students find it more difficult to . . .

- Be persuaded without data. They want proof that a new way will work before they accept it.
- Jump into new ideas until they are sure the idea will work.
- Brainstorm ideas without sufficient information.
- Understand the moods of others and how this impacts their choices.
- Learn when teachers rush the lesson.
- Make quick judgments without adequate information to support their choices.

Strengths & Stretches ISFJ

(Here and Now Helpers)

When ISFJs use their preferred style they . . .

- Are friendly with others and reach out to help them.
- Are responsible and do what needs to be done now.
- Take their work seriously.
- Are observant about people and their needs.
- Have a good memory for details that are necessary.
- Work persistently and thoroughly.
- Meet their commitments and obligations.

ISFJ students find it more difficult to . . .

- Tolerate others they think are selfish.
- Function in settings where rules change frequently.
- Learn when there is a lot of theory with no application.
- Continue to work in a setting where they feel unappreciated.
- Put their needs in front of the needs of others.
- Be assertive in expressing their opinion if they consider others experts.

Strengths & Stretches INFJ

(Insightful Humanist)

When INFJs use their preferred style they . . .

- Are warm and caring and sensitive to the needs of others.
- Get excited about learning what they are interested in knowing. They will work hard to learn all they need about topics that are important to them.
- Make plans easily and execute them well.
- Are dedicated to their values and will sacrifice much to meet their goals.
- Put the needs of others before their own most of the time.
- Take charge when they think others need direction.
- Enjoy playfulness and laugh heartily when the work is done.
- Have high ideals and standards that they want to share with others.

INFJ students find it more difficult to . . .

- Tolerate people who do not keep due date commitments.
- Wait until the last moment to begin a task.
- Accept that their plan will not be followed because someone failed to do their share.
- Learn that there are some things that cannot be managed, forcing them to adapt instead.
- Accept criticism from others when they are not secure in the relationship.
- Understand that their vision is not always what others see or want.

Strengths & Stretches INTJ

(Insightful Logicians)

When INTJs use their preferred style they . . .

- Are always looking for new challenges and something else to learn.
- Focus on the main idea and help others understand the concepts through their explanations.
- Are open to new ideas and new possibilities to solve problems.
- Use their self-confidence about what they know to take charge and lead others.
- Organize a task well and try to get it done; they tend to be efficient.
- Debate well and present their reasons for choices.
- Work well independently.

INTJ students find it more difficult to . . .

- Work with groups on a group project, especially, if they do not trust the skill level of all the members.
- Follow an idea that they think does not equal the quality of theirs.
- Remember numerous details that they did not consider relevant.
- Be sensitive to the feelings of others when they think they are right.
- Work in a nonstructured setting.
- Trust the advice of others unless they respect the giver's level of expertise on the topic.

Strengths & Stretches ISTP

(Realistic Problem Solvers)

When ISTPs use their preferred style they . . .

- Are sensible in the suggestions they offer to others.
- Work independently to meet personal objectives.
- Have a skill for understanding how things work.
- Enjoy hands-on work and use equipment well to help get the work done.
- See issues as problems to be solved and proceed to solve them.
- Express their ideas in clear and direct ways so others know their positions.
- Have a wealth of information available to clarify their ideas to others.
- Are quick to offer ideas based on their experience to help solve problems.

ISTP students find it more difficult to . . .

- Understand the emotions of others.
- Enjoy tasks that have little or no pragmatic value.
- Follow rules and a consistent routine. They like some diversity in the day.
- Accept ideas without sufficient details to support the statement.
- Find papers and materials unless they have a strategy for keeping track of them.

Strengths & Stretches ISFP

(Joyful Achievers)

When ISFPs use their preferred style they . . .

- Have a deep-felt caring for living things which often guides their choices.
- Show their compassion and care for others by what they do more than by what they say.
- Are sensitive to the emotional states and suffering of others.
- Are down-to-earth and focus on the here and now.
- Have an idealism that leads them to seek higher goals.
- Have a quiet, playful, and adventurous nature that others come to trust.
- Express a free kind of spontaneity that brings liveliness to the moment.
- Lead by focusing on the immediate need.

ISFP students find it more difficult to . . .

- Be bound by a lot of rules.
- Toot their own horns. They may undersell themselves.
- Forgive themselves for errors.
- Learn when the school work is rushed.
- Concentrate when there are many exciting things in the room to see and do.
- Make decisions when they are trying to do things perfectly.

Strengths & Stretches INFP

(Idealistic Helper)

When INFPs use their preferred style they . . .

- Are sensitive to the needs of others.
- Are motivated by what they hold to be important.
- Cooperate with the needs of the group.
- Willingly work hard to help others.
- Create new and divergent ways to accomplish work.
- Enjoy considering new ideas, but are best at refining old ideas in new ways.
- Are attracted to learning that focuses on people, their development, and relationships.
- Are usually seen as loyal, gentle, friendly, and quiet.

INFP students find it more difficult to . . .

- Accept their faults or accept when they are unable to do what is expected.
- Recall details unless told in advance this skill is expected.
- Present before a group of strangers unless they are sure of their topic.
- Work with others who are angry or fighting.
- Tell others when they are upset with them.
- Stand up to friends over minor things, although they can do so more easily with important issues.

Strengths & Stretches INTP

(Ingenious Questioner)

When INTPs use their preferred style they . . .

- Enjoy a chance to challenge themselves intellectually.
- Like to use their wit to make a point.
- Are good at talking about ideas, principles, and patterns.
- Like talking about a variety of complex issues. They can be very verbal about favorite topics.
- Are able to read between the lines.
- Can take complicated material and restate it in clear, simple ways.
- Set clear expectations for those who work with them, and they often help others maintain those standards.

INTP students find it more difficult to . . .

- Avoid jumping from topic to topic because they have a wide variety of interests.
- Doubt their decisions. They can trust their logic to the exclusion of listening to the reasons others present.
- See another person's point of view when it differs significantly from theirs.
- Follow through with the implementation of ideas because they are already on to something new.
- Tolerate people's questions or comments that they consider unimportant.
- Enjoy social interactions when they do not know the other people well.

Strengths & Stretches ESTP

(Action-focused Troubleshooter)

When the ESTPs use their preferred style they . . .

- Remember facts and information easily to help them with decisions.
- Are quick to see what is wrong with a situation.
- Are willing to take risks to try new projects or ideas.
- Make choices based on a logical analysis of the problem.
- Bring a lively spirit and a sense of playfulness to serious tasks.
- Are quick to analyze the best way to approach a problem.
- Are able to bring out the good in others through their casual approach.

ESTP students find it more difficult to . . .

- Sit and listen for long periods of time.
- Read as their only way of getting information. They want a chance to use the information.
- Tolerate systems that reward incompetent performances.
- Understand the main idea without good examples to support them.
- Keep to a routine and do things the same way each time if there are better options.
- Do their best when the directions are vague.

Strengths & Stretches ESFP

(Fun-loving Realists)

When ESFPs use their preferred style they . . .

- Are good at understanding people and respond to their needs.
- Bring a liveliness and spirit of fun while working on projects with others.
- Are eager to try new things once they understand the process.
- Are willing to work with and follow along with the group's decision.
- Are positive people who tend to see the sunny side of life.
- Are good at noticing details.
- Lead others with their fun-loving nature and their joy of doing.

ESFP students find it more difficult to . . .

- Learn without practicing. They understand things best when they get a chance to apply the learning to a real situation.
- Be in groups that argue a lot. They do not like working with people in conflict.
- Work in a highly structured room with a lot of rules. They prefer a loose structure with clear objectives.
- Work without playing and laughing, too.
- Recognize that their last-minute rush to finish may bother others.
- Sit still for long periods of time without something to touch or do.

Strengths & Stretches **ENFP**	Strengths & Stretches **ENTP**
(Energetic Humanists)	**(Enthusiastic Entrepreneur)**

When ENFPs use their preferred style they . . .

- Cultivate a wide network of friends.
- Are good conversationalists who make others feel comfortable.
- Get the main idea quickly.
- Are adventurers who encourage new experiences for the group.
- Want to be everywhere and do everything with and around people.
- Focus on the future and look for ways to improve the world for people.
- Serve as a catalyst for change while they generate enthusiasm in others for the task.
- Look for new and exciting ways to accomplish tasks.

ENFP students find it more difficult to . . .

- Recall details unless they know in advance the details are important.
- Study in quiet rooms or classrooms that rely mainly on workbooks or textbooks.
- Work without feedback or recognition for their contribution.
- Follow through and complete projects. Implementing an idea is not as easy for them as designing it.
- Stick with routine tasks unless the tasks are important to others they respect.
- Cope with tensions in their relationships.

When ENTPs use their preferred style they . . .

- Are entrepreneurial and innovative and can lead others to meet new challenges.
- Can take intellectually complex ideas and organize them into coherent connections.
- Use their ease with language to bring humor to the situation.
- Are quick to enjoy the challenge of resolving differing points of view.
- Find challenges exciting rather than threatening and lead easily in demanding times.
- Create and encourage change when change is an improvement.
- Have a high need for independence to solve problems that could then help others work better.

ENTP students find it more difficult to . . .

- Follow specific procedures and rules if they find these restrict them.
- Follow a group's momentum if the pace goes too slowly for them.
- Tune in to the emotional needs of others because they are focused on the task.
- Recall details unless they are advised in advance of that expectation.
- Follow through with producing something tangible from their ideas.
- Stick with a project from beginning to end because they are distracted by new ideas.

Strengths & Stretches ESTJ

(Pragmatic Decision Makers)

When ESTJs use their preferred style they . . .

- Collect a rich foundation of information to form the basis for their ideas.
- Focus on getting the job done and meet that objective.
- Organize materials and events well.
- Complete tasks quickly so they can get to the next task.
- Encourage others to keep working to get the job done well.
- Use logic to make sense of facts.
- Are ready and eager to make decisions and take action.
- Critique others and things that do not meet their standards. They offer this critique as information to help others.
- Willingly take charge of an event to help others maintain focus and follow the standard.

ESTJ students find it more difficult to . . .

- Work with people who they see as incompetent or indecisive.
- Yield to others to make the decision, especially if they need time to think first.
- Keep options open because they decide so quickly.
- Follow a random, theoretical discussion that has little practical value.
- Understand why they are wrong, unless new information is added.

Strengths & Stretches ESFJ

(Friendly Organizers)

When ESFJs use their preferred style they . . .

- Use their energy to resolve the needs of people and improve personal relationships.
- Seem to accurately sense what others feel or need.
- Appear warm and friendly to others and inspire cooperation in others.
- Use their experiences to increase their understanding.
- Help others plan their work.
- Have a strong sense of duty and follow through with their responsibilities.
- Get jobs done on time and help others to meet due dates, too.

ESFJ students find it more difficult to . . .

- Address conflict with others.
- Take care of their needs when others need their help.
- Sit for long periods of time with limited interaction.
- Listen for long periods of time without an opportunity to discuss the material.
- Process large units of information if they don't get a chance to use the information in some way.
- Follow along with teachers who seem to have a random method of instruction.

Strengths & Stretches ENFJ

(Cooperative Catalyst)

When ENFJs use their preferred style they . . .

- Get excited about ideas that help people.
- Are good at planning how to get a job done.
- Use their enthusiasm to entice others to share in the idea.
- Are good at talking out their ideas with others.
- Take responsibility seriously and try hard to meet their obligations.
- Plan ahead and like to follow their plan.
- Enjoy brainstorming new ways to solve problems that affect people.
- Interact easily with others on a social level.
- Inspire others through harmony and cooperation.
- Organize others well to get the job done.

ENFJ students find it more difficult to . . .

- Work with people they think are phony or fake.
- Be flexible on a moment's notice. They can be flexible after they think about it.
- Work when there is a lot of arguing or conflict.
- Tolerate team members goofing around while they work if the due date is close.
- Work with detailed tasks for a long period of time.
- Get excited about routines that become boring.
- Recall a lot of details unless they know in advance they will need to recall that information.

Strengths & Stretches ENTJ

(Logical Planner/Designer)

When ENTJs use their preferred style they . . .

- Have a keen eye for noticing what corrections need to be made that would save time and energy for others.
- Analyze and bring logic to a situation and can explain their thinking to others.
- Develop plans that move people to work more effectively.
- Know clearly what is right and wrong for them.
- Ask a lot of questions to sort information by importance.
- Like to take charge if people will let them lead.
- Plan so that the work gets done efficiently and effectively.
- Make goals and keep them.
- Connect information to ideas that lead to better choices.

ENTJ students find it more difficult to . . .

- Keep track of details unless they understand their importance to the result.
- Follow a plan that does not match the best way as they see it.
- Find time to complete all the ideas and designs they create.
- Work with people they consider incompetent.
- Tolerate mistakes others make.
- Wait and consider alternatives. Their eagerness to make a decision and finish may mean they miss good possibilities that might yet be considered.

Students need to both think
and feel that the classroom is a place
that honors their various styles.
Providing for differences means that
greater numbers of students will be
able to succeed in the classroom
environment.

5

Either/Or Language

Once you have an understanding of type descriptions for teachers and students, the next step is to use that information to allow each type to feel valued and acknowledged while continuing to meet the educational goals of the classroom. In addition to designing instructional presentations and assessment tools that allow differentiated approaches teachers can learn to incorporate choices into their language. Using choices in your language has several advantages. This strategy is called "either/or language" indicating that the teacher always offers a choice.

I really need to know every step, step-by-step. I'll try to ask questions politely and not be annoying.
(ISTJ)

When we adjust our explanation or our assessment to include choices based on type differences, we enhance a student's opportunity to understand the task and to complete it successfully.

Using language that gives others a type choice has three positive effects.

1. By providing a choice, you allow each student the opportunity to process information and make decisions in their preferred way.

2. By offering a choice, you demonstrate that there are many acceptable ways to meet the objective.

3. By including choices, you recognize that there are natural, good differences that need to be encouraged in any environment.

Either/Or Language Options

Following are just a few examples of either/or language to get you started. Phrase your questions or comments using choices based on type. For example, "Would you prefer to work alone or with friends on this task?"

Extraversion–Introversion

Would you prefer to . . .

• Work alone or with friends?

• Use a workbook first and then discuss or discuss and then use a workbook?

- Form thoughts aloud or form thoughts inside?

- Relax by doing or relax by resting alone?

- Share with many or share with close friends?

- Is this your final thought or your forming thought?

- Must talk when upset or can't talk when upset?

- Enjoy a quiet place to learn or enjoy an active place to learn?

Sensing–Intuition

Would you prefer to . . .

- Hear the details first or whole idea first?

- Receive complete directions or the gist of the directions in order to be successful?

- Have more examples or are these enough examples?

- Tell things in order from beginning to end or tell things in ways that are most interesting for you?

- Want the product to be useful or want the product to be innovative and different?

Thinking–Feeling

Would you prefer to . . .

- Consider the logic of a decision or the impact of the decision on others?

- Know the reasons why or know how this is important?

- Convince or persuade others?

- Help by solving the problem or help by listening?

- Say what you think is true or say what you think is needed?

- Know whether you did well or depend on others to give you feedback?

Judging–Perceiving

Would you prefer to . . .

- Play or practice?

- Work first or work when the need to get done is now?

- Plan ahead or adapt as needed to get done?

- Be prepared or be flexible with last minute ways?

- Work on one thing at a time or work on several things at a time?

- Put things away to be able to find them later or keep them out to be able to find them later?

6

Suggestions for Using Type Concepts

Teachers can use an awareness of type in many ways, including the following:

- Design lessons for different types of students.

- Understand differences in their coworkers and accommodate as needed.

- Use the language of differences to let students know that a variety of ways to accomplish a task will be honored.

On the following pages, you will find suggestions for accommodating type differences for students. These can be applied individually or with groups of students.

Once teachers have explored type concepts they can begin designing instruction and assessment to help different types of learners. The usual classroom impact of these designs is to increase achievement and to reduce the need for discipline.

I like to work alone, I get done faster. (ISTJ)

Knowing that I am an Extravert is helpful because I know that I just have to talk about it when I'm upset, it just helps me to cope. (ENTP)

Recommendations for Working with **Extraverted Students**

1. Provide opportunities for peer consultation approximately every 15 minutes. After delivering instruction for 15 minutes, let students turn to a partner and define what was just learned. This allows Extraverted students to verbalize the concepts, file them in memory, and be ready to receive additional input.

2. Extraverts are easily distracted by extraneous noises in the environment when they must concentrate. Provide a very quiet place when it is necessary for an Extraverted student to concentrate because of the difficulty of the task. If the work is not difficult, this is not an issue.

3. Allow Extraverted students to skim the chapter before the lecture and read it more thoroughly after the lecture or demonstration. Extraverts remember more if they thoroughly read the content after participating in the lecture or experiment.

4. Use conversation sticks (e.g. two pencils each) to help control the flow of conversation in small group sessions. After a student shares a thought, he must put a pencil in the middle of the table. When he has spent his two pencils, he must wait until all the members of the team have spent their two pencils before he can speak again. A student can spend a pencil by offering a new thought or by summarizing what has already been said.

5. Help Extraverted students form a network of acquaintances. Extraverts like to connect with many others as a research tool. They learn from being with groups.

6. Help Extraverted students pace the wait time. They may need hints to recognize that silence can mean that the other person is still thinking. Teach them to ask if the other person has an idea before they assume that silence means the other person has nothing to say.

7. Encourage Extraverts to take frequent small breaks in their work in order to help them regain the energy to continue to work independently.

8. Teach the Extraverted student how to hold a thought by jotting down an idea or an image that will help them recall what they were going to say if they do not have an opportunity to share immediately.

9. Teach younger Extraverted children how to use an internal "mute" button to stop expressing a thought out loud. They can mouth the words without making any sound. This allows them to participate without interfering with the thinking of others. Comparing it to the mute button found on the TV remote control seems to make the concept clear.

10. Recognize that the Extraverted student's first thoughts are not necessarily their final thoughts. Encourage them to talk through the ideas until they reach a final thought on the issue. Verbalizing helps an Extravert think better. When in doubt ask, "Is this your final thought or a thought still forming?"

Recommendations for Working with **Introverted Students**

1. Allow the Introvert a longer wait time between question and response.

2. Encourage an Introvert's conversation by making statements and then having a long pause between statements. Asking questions only encourages the Introvert to go back inside their head to consider an answer.

3. Use probing strategies to ask an Introvert's thoughts. In a group meeting or team meeting, Introverts may hesitate to interrupt. Others may interpret their waiting as not having a thought to offer. Ask each member of the team individually if they have questions or additional thoughts or comments to share. Asking the Introverted children directly gives them an opportunity to speak.

4. Use a nonverbal system (such as the red/green card) to allow the Introvert a procedure for nonverbally requesting assistance. Green means I am doing fine. Red means stop for a comment or question.

5. Recognize that an Introvert will remember more of a chapter if they read the text before the lecture or the demonstration. Pace the assignments to allow time for this opportunity.

6. Respect that when an Introvert shares an idea, there is usually a lot of thought behind it. If you have critical reservations about their choice, spend some time discussing the reasons behind their decision rather than attacking the final output.

7. Allow the Introvert an opportunity to sit alone for private reflection if the day has been busy and interactive. Introverts get their energy recharged by taking a few moments alone. Some Introverted children sit in front of the TV without really watching it as a way to get some time alone.

8. Teach the Introvert to give a signal or state that they are "still thinking." Often they take extra time to consider a thought but don't let the other person know they are still processing the task.

9. Validate that working with groups or working independently are both equal ways to choose to work. Introverts may feel socially isolated without the implicit or explicit endorsement of that style of working.

10. Set aside some quiet time for yourself in the classroom, which will allow Introverted children to have an opportunity to approach you with task or relationship questions.

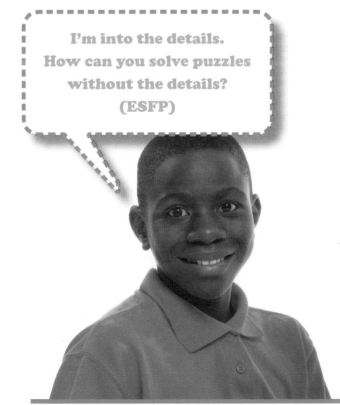

I'm into the details. How can you solve puzzles without the details? (ESFP)

Recommendations for Working with **Sensing Students**

1. Help the Sensing student sort relevant from irrelevant details. Initially all details seem important.

2. Provide a framework for organizing information that allows a Sensing student to enter the specific details first and then write the overall topic sentence.

3. Teach these students hierarchical ways to organize information to aid in recall.

4. Provide practice centers where students can retreat to repractice previously learned skills. Sensing types enjoy reviewing tasks they do well, especially just after they have learned it.

5. Allot more time for Sensing students to explore information and process it. This extra time is not related to ability. It is related to the joy that such students experience in thoroughly exploring all the pieces and the facts before looking for themes and connections.

6. Write directions to test questions or assignments with short sentences. List the tasks in order. The task can be complex, but the sentences explaining the directions should be brief and simple.

7. Allow the student to explore "what has worked in the past" as a first step toward problem solving. Sensing types value previous experience and build on that to discover new solutions.

8. Use experiential learning centers. Allow the student the opportunity to explore the parts of the microscope, for example. Explicitly state the learning expectation, for example, "name the parts of the microscope and their functions" or "describe five situations in which a microscope can be used."

9. Provide as many details to encourage the creativity of Sensing students, which is best stimulated when they have clear expectations and clear directions. Sensing types create from the known (specific) before going to the unknown (vague/general).

10. Allow the child to "word swap." The child can exchange a word that is motivating for one that is not motivating. For example, if the task is "create a model," some Sensing students may indicate that they do not want to "create" but would rather "make a model." The end product is the same, but the language used to motivate and produce the end product differs by type.

Recommendations for Working with **Intuitive Students**

1. Provide an overview of the content to be studied. Intuitive types need mental hangers for holding specific details.

2. Use a grading rubric so students understand the critical points that will be used for scoring a project or essay.

3. Allow students to complete a graphic organizer by putting in global themes followed by specific details. Intuitive types may list three or four themes before they begin identifying the specifics under each theme.

4. Teach students mnemonics for recalling specific information. Intuitive types do well with making connections and enjoy creating recall keys that are meaningful to them.

5. Allow the student to add words to explain what else would have been included on projects. This is especially important for the young Intuitive types, who may struggle to produce the designs they envision.

6. Let Intuitive type students know that they need to support their ideas with specific details by letting them know how many examples they should provide. Intuitive types frequently offer too few examples to demonstrate their point.

7. Understand that Intuitive types prefer limited directions so they can take the task in the direction they want. They feel freer to create with fewer directions.

8. Know that the natural energy of Intuitive types comes during the design phase. They are excited about generating possible ideas but may lose energy in producing the project. They may need mentor support to produce the ideas they conceive.

9. Help students frame their research. In the quest for information about a topic Intuitive types can begin to explore so many tangential topics that, in the end, they have a lot of information but limited depth to one topic.

10. Recognize that Intuitive types sometimes imagine they know more than they do. In their eagerness to explore new topics, they may rush through the learning details. Let them know the depth of learning required, so they know when to spend more time studying a topic.

Recommendations for Working with **Thinking Students**

1. Present issues as problems to be solved. Thinking students love to solve problems and will respond to that language.

2. Provide specific information about the student's grades and achievements. Thinking types value knowing where they stand compared to others in the class.

3. Appreciate that Thinking students thrive on personal challenges. Teach them to win fairly and lose graciously.

4. Readjust the standard of excellence to match the age of the student. Unless you establish the appropriate standard for age, these children will feel frustrated if they don't do well (e.g. if most ten-year-olds bowl 115, then the goal should be set at 115 rather than an adult perfect game of 300).

5. Thinking types prefer consistency in applying classroom rules and standards for all students, although they understand accommodations for children with special needs.

6. Know that Thinking students typically justify each answer. When challenged, they expect the other party to be able to defend their position. They naturally challenge those who disagree with them. This can create conflict when the Thinking child is talking with an adult.

7. Know that coping with incompetence is a struggle for Thinking students. When they are incompetent or fail at a task, they will sometimes blame others for their errors. In the intensity of the moment do not react to these comments. Instead, talk about their comments at a later time. More likely, a Thinking student will be able to listen more clearly when the embarrassment and frustration of the moment has passed.

8. Know that Thinking students require independence. They like to try things on their own and seem to resist when they have to ask permission.

9. Ask the Thinking student to identify what is wrong with a design or plan. They are quick to find the flaw in an idea.

10. Encourage Thinking students to attempt mental and strategic games such as chess, mind-benders, or Othello. This allows them to be able to compete against goals as well as against individuals.

Recommendations for Working with **Feeling Students**

1. Greet students daily. Feeling students like obvious connections with teachers in personal ways and need to know that the teachers are glad to see them each day.

2. Know that the Feeling student makes decisions based on values rather than logic. If their choice doesn't make sense, check to see what the underlying basis was for their choice. Most likely it was a value you did not appreciate or expect.

3. Understand that no feedback to a Feeling student is equal to a negative evaluation. If nothing is said the Feeling child will assume the other party did not value his or her contribution.

4. Understand that after you discipline a Feeling student, it's best to reassure him or her of your love, respect, or connection. The loss of the relationship is the greatest threat for Feeling students. Provide whatever consequence is needed but reassure them of the continued affiliation.

5. Help students learn how to resolve conflict. Feeling students especially may have a difficult time offering an apology. If they apologize and the other person does not accept the apology, they may, as a reaction, get angry with that person and feel twice rejected.

6. Help students find a cause to help. Feeling students have a strong need to provide service.

7. Recognize their need for affiliation. Feeling students need a group with which to identify. Independence can feel like loneliness for these children.

8. Help students learn to form a qualitative interpretation of the worth of their work. Feeling students tend to monitor adults and try to respond in ways they think will please adults or those in charge.

9. Know that when a task or a direction violates a Feeling student's values, they will adamantly refuse to comply. The values they hold trump the need to please the adult.

10. Accept that Feeling students are fiercely loyal to their friends and may find it difficult to tolerate criticism of those they embrace.

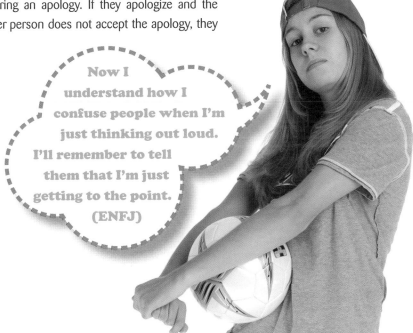

Now I understand how I confuse people when I'm just thinking out loud. I'll remember to tell them that I'm just getting to the point. (ENFJ)

Recommendations for Working with **Judging Students**

1. Provide a timeline for assignments. As much as possible do not vary from this timeline. Judging students count on the predictability of due dates.

2. Know that the Judging students like to make plans. Use this language such as the following when talking with them: "What is your plan for getting that accomplished?" and "What is your plan for solving that problem?"

3. Aid Judging students to develop flexibility by helping them create back-up plans. Rather than expecting them to become flexible, provide students with a pocket full of contingency plans to use if the original plan falls short or something interferes with its use. Having multiple contingency plans will honor their style and allow them to be flexible in a different way.

4. Avoid assigning multiple long-term projects due at the same time. Working against such pressure can be frustrating for the Judging students. Instead of being energized by the due date, they may become distressed and less effective. Children today have many commitments on their time, some work well at the last moment. However, for Judging students this is not a source of strength but a stretch and results in anxiousness and frustration.

5. Let Judging students know when the time for a project or activity is about to end. Knowing that the completion time is near allows them the opportunity to achieve closure. Students with a Judging preference are more comfortable bringing closure to one task before they begin a new one.

6. Understand that a crisis can be disconcerting to a Judging student unless they have a prepared way to handle the event. Thinking ahead of potential responses to possible emergencies can be helpful, for example, you might pose questions such as "What would you do if you got off the bus and mommy wasn't home yet?" or "What would you do if you were in the car with friends and they started drinking and driving?"

7. For younger students, reframe tattletales with "rule-clarifiers." Many young Judging children tattle on others as a way of checking out if the rule is a real rule that will be enforced. If some students are allowed to break a rule without justification, Judging types may feel the system is unfair. They will want to see the rules enforced for everyone. Judging children place high value on rules and on the enforcement of those rules.

8. Understand that Judging students can be full of fun and laughter once the work is done. They like to bring closure to tasks so they can have time to goof around and play. Laughing and playing while they work can be distracting for them. They may be irritated by Perceiving classmates who value the playful interactions while they are working.

9. Know that two Judging students can be in conflict if they have different plans or different schedules for completion of a task. Help students develop good timelines for when each person's contribution should be completed. Judging students typically plan their schedules to meet due dates.

10. Help the Judging student learn a plethora of coping skills. Judging students need to recognize that when they cannot control the event they must cope with the situation. Judgers are gifted with the sense of timing but must learn coping. Perceiving students are gifted with the sense of coping but must learn timing.

Recommendations for Working with **Perceiving Students**

1. Give the Perceiving child precise deadlines. Working at the last moment is more likely to produce their best thoughts. This is not procrastination. Procrastination is putting off doing tasks we don't want to do. Using the energy of the deadline to produce your work is a better description of the Perceiving student. Usually, they have been thinking and researching all along. They wait until the last moment to allow themselves the opportunity to consider all possible ideas until they absolutely have to decide.

2. Accept that Perceiving students are born without an internal sense of timing and must learn this skill. This means that they will likely underestimate how long a task will take. Then they will be pressed to complete it at the last moment. Teach them better timing rather than give a lecture on responsibility.

3. Understand that the Perceiving student combines work, laughter, and enjoyment. They like to make silly jokes or word-plays with the task at hand. Although they may look like they are clowning around they usually are actually on task. Judge them by their product rather than the style they used to produce the outcome.

4. Help Perceiving students pace their work by planning from the deadline backward. Say, "What is the last minute you can begin and still get this done?" Mention some possible interference that might encourage them to add a little lead time to their schedule.

5. Know that the strength of the Perceiving student is their adaptability. Rather than have a plan ready just in case like the Judging child, these children think best on the spur of the moment. They consider any plan as tentative until the event passes.

6. Appreciate that the Perceiving student can come up with the best ideas in a moment of crises. Allow them opportunities to lead when no plan is in place.

7. Use the comment, "Good act, bad timing" to redirect a student who gets a little too silly with a task. The ESP student is sometimes an actor or performer who loves to entertain others on their team. This performance can be disconcerting to a Judging child who wants to complete tasks before enjoying the moment.

8. Understand that the Perceiving student has no true need to complete all the projects they begin. Just experiencing a part of the task is sometimes sufficient.

9. Use words as "play" or "experience" or "attempt" to motivate Perceiving students. Words such as "work", "practice", or "should" generally discourage Perceiving children.

10. Know that some Perceiving students live moment to moment (EP) and these students can sometimes lose track of materials, books, important papers, etc. Have a specific place to put materials each day so the students know to look there as a first choice. Again, lectures of responsibility are rarely effective. Instead problem solve to develop a strategy to keep track of items. The student's preference for Intuition or Sensing will contribute to the development of the best plan for them.

Comments from Children About Type

Students were asked to make comments about how an understanding of type influenced them. The following is a sample of their reactions.

"Knowing that I am an Extravert is helpful because I know that I just have to talk about it when I'm upset, it just helps me to cope." (ENTP)

"Now I understand how I confuse people when I'm just thinking out loud. I'll remember to tell them that I'm just getting to the point." (ENFJ)

"I like to work alone, I get done faster." (ISTJ)

"I really need to know every step, step-by-step. I'll try to ask questions politely and not be annoying." (ISTJ)

"I know I like to do things my way with little instruction. I learn stuff in different ways; I will try harder to follow the teacher's way." (INTP)

"I'm into the details. How can you solve puzzles without the details?" (ESFP)

"I'm a Feeling person, maybe I shouldn't be so gullible." (ENFP)

"I enjoy competition. I will try to have more fun while I'm competing and not be so serious about it so my friends won't get mad." (ESTJ)

"It's hard for me to think when a deadline is near and the project isn't done." (ESTJ)

"No matter what my mom says, 'Work now, play later' is an opinion." (ENTP)

Further Reading

Barger, J. R.; R. R. Barger; and J. M. Cano. 1994. *Discovering learning preferences and learning differences in the classroom.* Ohio State University, Columbus, OH: Ohio Agricultural Education Curriculum Materials Service.

DiTiberio, J. and G. H. Jensen. 1995. *Writing and personality.* Palo Alto, CA: Davies-Black Publishing.

Ellison, L. 1993. *Seeing with magic glasses.* Arlington, VA: Great Ocean Publishers.

Fairhurst, A. and L. Fairhurst. 1995. *Effective teaching effective learning.* Palo Alto, CA: Davies-Black Publishing.

Farris, D. 2000. *Type tales.* Gainesville, FL: Center for Applications of Psychological Type.

Gibbs, J. 1987. *Tribes: A process for social development and cooperative learning.* Santa Rosa, CA: Center Source Publications.

Golden, B. J. and K. Lesh. 1994. *Building self-esteem.* Scottsdale, AZ: Gorsuch Scarisbrick Publishers.

Hirsh, S. and J. Kummerow. 1989. *Lifetypes.* New York: Warner Books.

Kise, J. 2006. *Differentiated coaching: A framework for helping teachers change.* Thousand Oaks, CA: Corwin Press.

Kise, J. 2007. *Differentiation through personality styles.* Thousand Oaks, CA: Corwin Press.

Kroeger, O. and J. Thuesen. 1988. *Type talk.* New York: Delacorte Press.

Lawrence, G. 1993. *People types and tiger stripes: A practical guide to learning styles,* 3rd edition. Gainesville, FL: Center for Applications of Psychological Type.

Lawrence, G. 1997. *Looking at type and learning styles.* Gainesville, FL: Center for Applications of Psychological Type.

Murphy, E. 1992. *The developing child.* Palo Alto, CA: Davies-Black Publishing.

Myers, I. B. with P. B. Myers. 1995. *Gifts differing,* 2nd edition. Palo Alto, CA: Consulting Psychologist Press.

Pearson, C. 1991. *Awakening the heroes within.* San Fransicco: HarperSanFrancisco.

Penley, J. P. 2006. *MotherStyles using personality type to discover your parenting strengths.* Cambridge, MA: Da Capo Press (www.motherstyles.com).

Piirto, J. 1992. *Understanding those who create.* Dayton, OH: Ohio Psychology Press.

VanSant S. and D. Payne. 1995. *Psychological type in schools: Applications for educators.* Gainesville, FL: Center for Applications of Psychological Type.

Wickes, F. G. 1927. *The inner world of childhood.* Englewood Cliffs, NJ: Prentice-Hall, Inc.

NOTES

_____

_____

_____

_____

_____

_____

_____

_____

_____

_____

_____

_____

_____

_____

_____

_____

_____

_____

_____

_____

_____

_____

_____

_____

_____

_____

_____

_____

_____

_____

_____

_____

NOTES

_____

_____

_____

_____

_____

_____

_____

_____

_____

_____

_____

_____

_____

_____

_____

_____

_____

_____

_____

_____

_____

_____

_____

_____

_____

Elizabeth Murphy (INFP)
AUTHOR

Elizabeth is a psychologist who has worked with type concepts since the early 1980s. Her research focuses on verifying (with video support) the development of normal personality differences according to the theory of psychological type. She works extensively with families and teams of people to improve communication and resolve relationship needs. She is an internationally recognized educational authority, whose experience includes conducting training throughout the United States as well as Canada, Singapore, Australia, New Zealand, and Malaysia. Her contribution to and leadership in developing the MMTIC™ assessment reflects her unusual and diverse educational background. She has taught children from preschool to high school age and worked as a licensed school psychologist. She is also the author of *The Developing Child*. Her dissertation won the Isabel Briggs Myers research award, and she received the Gordon Lawrence award for contributions to type in education. Carlow College honored her with their Alumna Award. Currently, she works as an independent consultant to schools and organizations and families.